LEVERAGE LIVESTREAMING TO BUILD YOUR BRAND

leverage

verb

1. use (something) to maximum advantage.

livestreaming

verb

1. transmitting or receiving live video and audio coverage over the Internet

brand

noun

1. a product manufactured or service provided by a particular company under a particular name

2. how a person or business is perceived by others based on information that is presented both on and off the internet

monetize

verb

1. convert or express in the form of currency
2. earn revenue from

from **Jenny** ⬛ **Live.com**

Foreword by Bryan Kramer

LEVERAGE LIVESTREAMING
TO BUILD YOUR BRAND

Start, Master, and Monetize Live Video

With Insider Tips & Tricks

by JENNIFER QUINN

Leverage Livestreaming to Build Your Brand: Start, Master, and Monetize Live Video
© 2018 NYO Media & Publishing, LLC
http://JennyQLive.com

Cover design: Tiffany Eller
Photography: JWolfe Productions
Hair & Makeup: Kelsi Jo Baker

Published by WIPublish
A Division of Women Ignite International
Boise, ID
www.womenigniteinternational.com

~ Dedicated to the livestreaming community ~

It truly does take a village, thank you for being mine

Table of Contents

Foreword

Not only is Jennifer Quinn a livestreaming superstar, she's also a great friend of mine who's always bursting with innovative and creative ideas, while championing new, exciting ways to connect with people. I'm sure you'll agree that the friends that challenge your thinking and bring insightful perspectives to the table are definitely the best kind...and ace dinner party guests too.

When JennyQ Is around – things always get interesting, so I feel super stoked to introduce her book and share a little bit about why it's unmissable.

As someone who's always looking for the most effective forms of human-centric marketing, livestreaming jumps out at me as the perfect tool to show off your brand's personality and authentic voice. I'm the founder of the Human to Human marketing movement and I spend lots of time writing, promoting and chatting about the benefits of honest, meaningful relationships with customers. It's what I do and when I find other people that totally get that idea and endorse tools that embody the same humanizing ethos – well, you can count me in.

Jennifer is an incredibly astute, pioneering marketer and she's passionate about communicating how you can use livestreaming as a cornerstone of your brand's marketing strategy to build a loyal customer base.

Whether you're looking to build your authority with a personal brand, take your new business venture to the next level, attract the best new talent, re-brand your marketing strategy or just love having a dialogue with your audiences– this one's for you.

Livestreaming is still a relatively fresh concept and its dramatic upsurge is in part due to the fantastic content creators that use it to produce their personalized output and also the behind-the-scenes marketers who push its benefits.

Pivoting your digital presence toward video content is a very shrewd move. After all, these young whipper snappers we like to label Generation Z, are going to consume more and more video content, especially on mobile. They're digital natives with an annual purchasing power of $44bn – meeting them on the platforms that they hang out on is crucial. You wouldn't want to miss the boat on this one, would you? Video rules and your brand should prepare for the connection, dynamism and rapid reactions that Generation Z is used to.

Enter – livestreaming.

With Jennifer's guidance and on-the-money commentary, you'll learn why livestreaming is the next best thing you can adopt for your brand and how you can maximize your ROI by creating long-lasting and meaningful relationships with customers. Become confident about launching live video on any number of platforms, from Facebook Live,

YouTube Live, Twitter, Periscope and Instagram. JennyQ is perfectly positioned to show small businesses how to embrace livestreaming and get creative.

From the technology you'll need to create informative and entertaining live videos to the techniques you can use to produce engaging, personality-packed content – JennyQ will walk you through her tips, tricks and know-how.

Jennifer's book is packed full of her entrepreneurial experience, with loads of examples and case-studies to illustrate how brands and entrepreneurs have harnessed livestreaming to build their business. She'll show you how it's not just digital stores and brands that are best placed to livestream - brick-and-mortar businesses can also join the party and monetize their vids and show off new products.

If your brand doesn't pivot towards more video content, your brand could easily fall behind. It makes business sense to implement livestreaming into your digital strategy and as JennyQ highlights - it's low risk and high reward. After years of intense involvement in livestreaming tech, learn from the best with Jennifer's years of experience, expertly illustrated with this highly informative and engaging book.

Bryan Kramer

Bestselling Author, Keynote & TED speaker, and CEO

Introduction

"A year from now you will either be the most brilliant person or the biggest fool ever," he said. This was during a phone conversation with my friend and colleague, Tobe Brockner.

It was 2015 and I was doing a daily show on a livestreaming platform, interviewing people who demonstrate excellence in their field. Tobe was watching me devote 45 minutes per day live online to conduct these interviews, not counting the amount of time it took to prepare, coordinate, and promote.

While it was true that I was distracted from building my digital marketing business to pursue this new technology, the last thing I felt like was a fool.

"That will never be the case," I told Tobe. "No matter what happens, I am making real human connections, learning a lot, and having fun. How can that ever equate to being a fool?"

Over two years later, I couldn't help myself.

I had to ask him.

"Now that you've seen it all unfold, what do you think?"

He said, "Well, it's not often we get to see someone spot a trend and jump on it before the big players do...but seeing how Facebook, YouTube, and others are throwing big dollars and resources at livestreaming, you look brilliant!"

When I started livestreaming in 2015, there was not a book guiding me through it — I learned everything through trial and error, and admittedly, there were a lot of errors! But now, I'm here to guide you, step-by-step, and help you avoid some of the common mistakes made by new livestreamers. I'm also going to help you get over the worries that all newbies have and take you from FEAR to FABULOUS in no time!

How It All Began:

Based on my informal straw poll of my international collection of Facebook friends, Boise, Idaho, is known for a lot of things. Among them are the Boise River, the Greenbelt along the river, tubing down the river, fishing, lakes, hunting, the blue football turf at Boise State University (which we affectionately call the Smurf Turf), snow, hiking trails, skiing, and of course, potatoes.

According to my "research," one thing that Boise is not known for is technology. So, how did it happen, that I, a small business owner in Boise, Idaho, became involved with the new technology of livestreaming? And more importantly, what have I learned from it?

It all started in March 2015. Someone suggested I try a new livestreaming app called Periscope. When she showed it to me I was underwhelmed. I wasn't quite sure why I would want to watch a man in Los Angeles talk to his phone while hundreds of people tapped the screen to send him virtual hearts and make comments in hopes that he would read them aloud or give them a shout out. All I could think was, "Don't these people have a life?"

Jennifer Quinn

Although I had owned a marketing business since 2007, and had an affinity with social media (especially Twitter!), I simply didn't get how livestreaming would be a "thing," nor did I see how anyone could use it for business! That's laughable now!

Then in July 2015, another friend suggested that I would "just love" Periscope. I asked him why, and he opened his phone to show me. I wondered what people were finding so fascinating about livestreaming, so I gave it more of a serious look. I didn't have time during my day to play around with it, so instead of watching television to unwind at night, I would open the Periscope app and watch people's broadcasts or "scopes."

And then it happened.

In the wee hours of the morning I landed on Josh Greenbaum's scope. He was broadcasting from New Jersey, and there was something about his genuine care for his viewers that captured my attention. There he was, a twenty-something guy, working full-time in a clothing store by day and was a Periscope personality by night. I watched him interact with his hundreds of viewers and saw how they were responding by their live comments. Josh was making a real connection with people on the other side of the screen. They were sharing intimate details with him, and they were being heard! I felt it at that moment: lives were being changed, one livestream at a time.

At that point, I was hooked. One might even say addicted! Every free moment I had, I logged on to the app to see what people were doing. I couldn't get enough of all the different ways people were using this new medium.

Only a few days in, I came across a millennial out of Connecticut named Vincenzo Landino. It turns out he was one of the top livestreamers and was heading up a national campaign for Applebee's. The campaign started the following day, and it called for broadcasters from locations all over the country to scope from their local Applebee's to promote the new menu and talk about the free samples that were being given out that day.

The idea of being a part of something utilizing this new technology was just too exciting. So, even though Vincenzo had no idea who I was, I took the chance and reached out by sending a comment into the Periscope stream. It looked something like this:

"Do you have anyone in Boise, Idaho?"

Nothing. Vincenzo kept talking about the upcoming promotion.

"Do you have anyone from the Boise, Idaho, Applebee's broadcasting?" I commented again.

Vincenzo tried to ignore me, but I really wanted to learn all I could about livestreaming and be a part of this new way of marketing.

"Do you have anyone from Boise, Idaho, to go live?" I asked a third time.

"JennyQ, no, we don't. Send me a Twitter DM," he finally said.

I sent the Twitter DM (direct message) and Vincenzo replied. The rest, as they say, is history. It's funny now to hear Vincenzo tell the story. He says, "I was wondering who this lady was from Boise, Idaho. She just wouldn't stop!" Then he adds, "I didn't expect to ever hear from her. I tell so many people to DM me, and they never follow through."

Long story short, I got the information from Vincenzo, and although I made so many newbie mistakes, I became totally hooked on live video. The Applebee's campaign was a groundbreaking international event bringing live feeds from the United States, Scotland, and England. On the day of the event there were over 15,000+ live viewers and the entire campaign had 39.5 million viewers in reach.

In August 2015, while watching a Periscope broadcast by Joanne Pham, founder of the PeriGirls, I was introduced to another livestreaming platform called Blab. The format was different than Periscope: I logged on to the Blab app from my laptop and found that in this platform one could have up to four people on screen at a time. Unlimited viewers could watch and comment live.

My first time on Blab the thought came to me as an intuitive hit, "I need to start interviewing people! I need to do a show where I interview people who demonstrate excellence in their fields." I started the daily show within a week, but before I started my first show, I had another intuitive hit, "Do the show, and **personal growth will come**. Do that, too." At the time I thought, "Okay," having no idea how this would profoundly affect my life.

Within six months I was voted "Queen of Blab", and a year later I started "Facebook Live's First Variety Show." I've conducted over 350 live interviews including author Bob Burg of "The Go Giver," author don Miguel Ruiz, Jr.

of "The Five Levels of Attachment," and Judge Alex from "Judge Alex TV." On every show, with every interview, I was left feeling inspired and motivated to do better, be better, and do more.

Livestreaming attracts such a diverse group of people - in regular life we tend to stick with people who have similar interests, the same belief systems, and who are in the same socioeconomic status. But, with livestreaming, people from all walks of life hopped on the app and hit "Start Broadcast."

I've heard that two types of people were attracted to the early days of livestreaming - narcissists and empaths. Ha! I don't know if that's true, but I do know that I have met some of the most amazing people in my life.

What I couldn't have predicted is how the livestream journey would change me and my business! Since I started livestreaming, Klout has named me the #2 Livestreaming Expert worldwide. I have worked with a production company as the Program Manager, onboarding big brands as they launch their professionally produced livestreaming shows.

I am passionate about helping businesses and individuals get their product, service, offering, or story of inspiration out into the world! I have seen lives change because of something seen or connections made on a live video broadcast.

The really exciting part of this is that livestreaming is still in its pioneering phase. We have not hit critical mass with businesses and brands using it as a marketing tool. We are still at the ground floor. The time is now, and the opportunity is prime for you to jump on board!

If you have any questions as you read this book, or if you want to get more insider tips and tricks, please connect with me in my Facebook group and ask them! It's a great community where everyone learns and everyone wins! Simply go to Facebook.JennyQ.Live to join us!

SECTION 1:
WHAT, WHY, WHO,
AND WHERE
OF LIVESTREAMING

JennyLive.com

Chapter 1:
What Is Livestreaming?

Livestreaming is a technology that allows you to broadcast something in real time from your location and push it out to a live, interactive audience. It's a really quick, easy way to connect with others from all over the world. And if you're a business owner, entrepreneur, or solopreneur, it's an effective way to connect with your customers, too. We'll talk a little bit more about that later.

The opportunity is unprecedented, as we now have the power at our fingertips, through our mobile device, to literally reach people from all over the world with our message, products, or services.

You are likely familiar with live broadcasts from traditional media, such as news coverage, live sporting events, award shows, and live concerts. The concept of broadcasting live isn't new. What IS new is the power that we have as individuals to simply open an application from our mobile device or our computer and show what we are doing, our thoughts, our businesses, or anything we want to share with the world! Doing it this way is now called "livestreaming," and the power is right there in your cellphone and computer, instead of at the headquarters of some big broadcasting company.

While livestreaming has been available to individuals since as far back as 2011 with the YouNow app, and first appearing within Snapchat in 2014, it really began to hit mainstream in January 2015 when Twitter acquired Periscope. Periscope is a mobile application that originated on iOS, then launched on Android three months later. Seemingly overnight, people from all around the world were connecting by simply picking up their phone and hitting the "Start Broadcast" button.

It didn't take long for the big social media players to realize that they were losing a big share of digital traffic by not being in the live video world: Enter Facebook and YouTube. If you're on any of those platforms, you know that they are vying to be the number one livestreaming platform by pushing out live video to larger audiences. You probably see that live videos are now a large portion of the posts in your newsfeeds. This is because the algorithms are designed to serve live video more often than any other content. This preferential treatment is a big reason to jump in to livestreaming. No other format is given such preference by Big Media.

In the next chapter, I share some compelling statistics on how live video increases engagement on social media, and why it is such a powerful tool for businesses, brands, and entrepreneurs.

Chapter 2:
Why Is Livestreaming So Hot Right Now?

When I started my marketing company in 2007, Facebook was three years old and had just launched the mobile version of their application. The website was still primarily used by college students wanting to connect. At the same time, Twitter had been around for a year and was building up steam as their users began seeing huge value in making business connections.

By 2012, I pivoted my company from a traditional marketing emphasis to a digital marketing emphasis. As I would speak to clients and groups, the question I would hear the most often was, "What is the ROI (return on investment) of social media?" And I would tell them, "You get to still be in business in five years!"

I now believe the same is true of livestreaming. If you want to still be in business in five years, the time is now to jump on the livestreaming train.

All of social media, livestreaming included, is about building relationships. While sales are definitely made via these modalities, the long game - and the real ROI - is based on creating, developing, and nurturing relationships.

If you get nothing else from this book, please get the above paragraph. It honestly is the entire reason to even consider incorporating livestreaming into your marketing strategy.

We all know that people do business with those they know, like, and trust. Live video is a tool that catapults the know, like, and trust factor like nothing we've ever seen before.

No longer can people or brands hide behind perfectly polished logos, commercials, websites or social media profiles. Consumers are coming to expect to get to know the people behind the brand on a more intimate level. Authenticity matters. In a time where fraudulent marketing is so common, and much of our world is changing so fast, we try to figure out whom we can trust.

Livestreaming is an ideal medium to convey this personal trust.

Livestreaming is like a magnifying glass on life. If you are a great person, or if your company has an amazing mission, or if your product serves people in a way that changes lives, it's going to show up on live video infinitely greater than what you can portray with a simple ad, image or text alone.

A study done in 2016 by BI Intelligence (Business Insider's research service), examined livestreaming video from the perspective of consumers and advertisers, assessing how live video is exceeding conventional marketing standards. The results were compelling.

Some key takeaways from the report:

- Livestreaming video will further accelerate streaming video's overall share of internet traffic. Streaming video accounts for *over two-thirds* of all internet traffic, and this share is expected to jump to *82%* by 2020, according to Cisco's June 2016 Visual Networking Index report.
- Live video's value comes from its unique ability to add an authentic human element to digital communications. As a result, brands are leveraging three main streaming methods to connect with their

viewers: tutorials, product launches, and exclusive behind-the-scenes footage.

- Advertisers will continue to invest heavily in online video, especially as livestreaming video gains traction. In the US, digital video ad revenue reached $7.8 billion in 2015, up 55% from 2014, according to figures from the Internet Advertising Bureau.
- While livestreaming is still in its early stages, brands are leveraging micropayments, mid-roll video ads, and direct payments from social platforms to monetize their livestreaming videos.
- The success of livestreaming video hinges on brands overcoming a lack of measurement standards in the space, as well as changes in social media sites' algorithms that affect what content users see.

(For information source, see: http://www.businessinsider.com/youtube-monetizes-live-streams-with-super-chat-2017-1)

Alex Khan, a successful German businessman, has used livestreaming to grow his business and his personal brand. Recently he shared this in a Facebook post:

150 Million Reasons for Live Video – Alex Khan

Many people ask me if they should spend time and money to invest in live video. As far as I am concerned, I gained 400,000 followers, got featured in Forbes and the Huffington Post, and built another business based on the power of live video.

Can I guarantee that you will do the same? For sure NOT, but here are some powerful facts.

Did you know that Twitter invested $100 million in live video by acquiring Periscope two years ago?

Facebook invested $50 million by paying celebrities to use live video. Every fifth video that is uploaded on Facebook is live.

And there are many more social networks like YouTube and Live.Me that are heavily investing in this new technology.

Please take one moment and ask yourself if you think you are more clever than Twitter, Facebook, or YouTube?

I leave it up to you to decide that.

It's not about asking yourself when is the right moment to jump on the boat: Be the engine that drives the ship forward!

It is predicted that **by 2019, 85% of all web traffic will be video.**

Here are some other impressive stats from http://telescope.tv:

- *80%* of people would rather watch live video from a brand than read a blog
- On average, people watch a live video *more than three times* longer when it is live compared to on-demand video
- People watch *42.8 minutes* for live video content versus *5.1 minutes* for on demand
- On average, people comment on Facebook live videos *10 times more* than regular video
- *1 in 5* Facebook users watch live video
- Most watched live content:
  - 56% breaking news
  - 44% conferences and speakers
  - 44% concert and festivals
- Live video consumption *grew 81%* between 2015 and 2016

- *87%* of audiences go online for behind-the-scenes access and to interact with talent
- *45% of audiences would pay* for live exclusive content, such as live performers or on-demand video with favorite teams
- Viewers spent *eight times longer* with live video than on-demand
- Facebook's algorithm *prioritizes longer live videos*
- Live video on social generates *12,000% more shares* (no that's not a typo) than text and images combined
- *67%* of live video viewers are more likely to buy a ticket to a concert or event after watching a live video of that event or a similar one
- As brands compete for eyeballs in the newsfeed, live video is a key differentiator
- Live video is outpacing the growth of other types of online video with *113% increase in growth* yearly
- *82%* preferred live video from a brand to social posts

Chapter 3:
Who Should Be Using Live Video?

As I mentioned earlier, anyone who wants to be in business in five years should be using live video. That is a pretty broad statement, so let's dive into the specifics of who should be using this exciting new medium. Anyone who:

- Wants to increase their know, like, and trust factor
- Wants to stand out from the crowd
- Wants to differentiate themselves as a brand
- Wants to be an early adopter or pioneer
- Is not afraid to learn a new technology
- Likes to make a difference
- Is looking for innovative marketing solutions
- Finds it easier to talk than to write
- Has a message to share with the world

- Is looking for new ways to attract customers

The list could go on, really. But let's look closer at who could benefit from livestreaming for their brand or business.

1. Small Business Owners

Having come from a long line of entrepreneurs, I have a soft spot in my heart for the small business owner. This makes me especially excited about the use of live video to help the small business owner stand out from the crowd!

A common misconception on using live video is that it can't benefit a traditional brick-and-mortar business. In reality, the use of livestreaming is only limited by a lack of ideas and creativity.

When I think of a great example of how livestreaming can transform a brick-and-mortar business, I think of John Kapos, also known as "Chocolate Johnny." John Kapos is a 3rd generation chocolatier and is the owner of Perfection Chocolates in Sydney, Australia.

Chocolate Johnny has embraced livestreaming as a way to let people get to know him and to also get a behind-the-scenes glimpse of what really happens in a chocolate factory. In addition to showing how different types of chocolates are made, Chocolate Johnny keeps his audience engaged in a variety of ways. He is constantly creating livestreaming experiences for his viewers, developing story lines with imagined "Oompa Loompas" and taking his viewers to the beach during gorgeous Australian sunsets.

As a result of livestreaming, Perfection Chocolates has gone from just a local iconic Australian business to an international phenomenon. Chocolate Johnny often goes live from his brick-and-mortar business with travelers from across the globe who heard about him and his business from watching his livestream broadcasts.

2. Personal Brands

Livestreaming is arguably the greatest technology to come along for helping build a personal brand. Where else can you interact on a one-to-many basis and connect on a real, human level? Personal connection is within the very nature of livestreaming.

To build a personal brand, one should follow these guidelines on live video:
- Show who you really are – be authentic

- Show up consistently
- Show up in a way that people expect to see you – this builds trust
- Engage with people on your live feeds – respond to comments
- Share a lot – but don't over share – it's a balancing act
- Be vulnerable – people truly want to connect with realness. Realness engenders credibility in a predominantly fake world

Livestreaming can boost your national and international visibility. As you build an audience of people who are interested in your information, products, services, or offerings, it's unpredictable where it might lead!

For example, take Hilary Silver. As a private practice therapist from Denver, Colorado, she grew a following and got the attention of "The Steve Harvey Show," syndicated nationally on television. I met Hilary in San Francisco in January of 2016 at the Summit Live conference. Since then, she has been a guest on my show several times sharing her expertise on relationships, love, and sex. I asked her to give us a summary of how livestreaming changed her life and her business.

SUCCESS STORY: From Private Practice to the Steve Harvey Show – with Livestreaming

I started private practice as a therapist in Denver in 2003. Although it was successful, about 3-4 years ago I started to feel an itch to do more. Seeing just one person at a time made it challenging to continue growing my business. Plus, I started paying attention to the fact that I was repeating myself over and over. In my experience, hearing story after story after story- up to thousands- what I know to be true is if it's an experience one of us has had, it's an experience many of us have had. I had started thinking about writing a book, or public speaking (which at the time scared me to death). Live video wasn't even a thing- it didn't exist in the mainstream at all.

Then in July of 2015, I discovered this app called Periscope! I downloaded it. I opened it up. I clicked on somebody. And suddenly they were talking to me through their screen to mine. It was so cool. I then put it down because it was early in the morning and I was headed out on my run.

When I got home, I grabbed my phone. I sat on the front porch, with red cheeks and still-sweaty hair. Without any notes, I hit the "start broadcast" button to share some thoughts I had and see what would happen.

And my life and business changed forever! I didn't know what I was doing but the viewers responded positively anyway. I was hooked.

I started broadcasting at the same time every day. I had a daily "show" where I shared my knowledge and content. I was making connections like crazy- both with clients and with other broadcasters, some of which are now my close friends. My life and my business exploded. My social media platforms grew, and I was a speaker at the Periscope Summit in San Francisco.

Within one year almost to the day, I grew enough brand visibility that I was noticed and recruited by a media company. Within two years, I had gone from a local brick-and-mortar online "nobody," to thousands of followers on Twitter, Periscope and Facebook, my first appearance on the Steve Harvey Show, interviews on the EOFire podcast, and other media like Inc., Fox News, Women's Health, Men's Fitness, and Martha Stewart's Weddings.

3. Big Brands

Since people want to connect with people, and people do business with those they know, like, and trust, what better way to humanize your brand than to use live video and allow people to get a glimpse of what it's like to work with your employees in a one-on-one way?

One of my favorite examples of how a big brand used livestreaming was done by Dunkin' Donuts. They hopped on the live video train early on. Of the specific livestream broadcasts that I saw, here are a few things they did that made it so successful:

1. To represent the brand, they chose employees who were personable, relatable, likable, and knowledgeable.
2. They had an interesting topic and showed viewers a few different areas of headquarters so people could get a behind-the-scenes look.
3. It was scripted, but not tightly so. There was an outline of the format, but the on-air broadcasters were able to still ad-lib, interact with the viewers and each other, and have spontaneity. You could tell that these were real people. And real people are trustable and fun to do business with.

4. Authors/Speakers/Coaches

I've tried to think of a more competitive category than this, and I can't. For decades, authors, speakers, and coaches have invested countless hours and thousands of dollars in having the best authority websites, and marketing their products/services via social media. In fact, the more I think about it, the more I realize that livestreaming is probably a dream come true for people in this category!

Livestreaming allows authors, speakers, and coaches to shine in their gifts and share their unique spin on what they do with the masses. Live video allows them to really connect and engage with perspective clients and customers. It alleviates any doubt and removes objections in short order because the client can see firsthand how a coach or speaker engages in real time.

With live video, there is no post-production polish or editing out the bloopers. This is truly what sets livestreaming apart from any other type of marketing tools.

Picture the scene from the classic "The Wizard of Oz," where the curtain is pulled to reveal the real person behind the imagined "Wizard – Knower and Seer of All Things" persona. You see human vulnerabilities, and while with the wizard it might have cost him his position, in the business world, what that does is it makes you more relatable, likable, and trustworthy.

Imagine you are seeking a speaker for your next event. It's likely you will start your search on LinkedIn looking for people who have "keynote speaker" in their profile. When you narrow the field down to a handful of people with expertise in your topic, in addition to checking out their profile, recommendations, and previous speaking engagements, you would probably then watch their speaker sizzle-reel.

Assuming you found three or four possible candidates from your initial search who could fit the speaker requirements perfectly, how would you make your decision?

As you look further into each possible candidate, you come across some livestreams on their Facebook business page, or some Periscope broadcasts in their Twitter feed. Within no time, you are able to get a truer sense of what each speaker will bring to your event. You're able to see how each candidate responds in real time to comments from viewers, engagement with other people on the broadcasts, and the inevitable errors that happen in livestreaming.

5. Professionals

A large component of professional services depends on personal credibility. When a person is looking for someone to trust with their health, legal issues, insurance needs, or financial questions, they want someone with whom they have a personal connection and solid trust. It can take several in-person visits to establish the kind of trust needed in these critical business relationships.

Livestreaming can dramatically decrease the time needed to build trust and rapport for those in professional industries, including: lawyers, certified public accountants, engineers, doctors, insurance agents, counselors, financial advisors, massage therapists, and chiropractors, just to name a few.

One such professional, attorney Mitch Jackson of Orange County, California, is a great example of how to use livestreaming to build trust, rapport, and business. I first saw Mitch on Periscope and was thrilled to meet him in real life in New York City in September 2015 at the first Periscope Summit. Because of the power of live video, when Mitch and I met in person, it felt more like seeing an old friend than making an acquaintance for the first time. Instead of an awkward introduction and stiff handshake, we were smiling and greeted each other with a hug. That's the power of livestreaming! To coin an old jingle from a 1970's television advertisement for Bell Systems – "It's the next best thing to being there!"

Mitch has been an early adopter of technology and social media, so when livestreaming became an option, he not only embraced it, but he became a trusted member of the livestreaming community by offering legal, social media, business, and livestreaming tips on his website http://Streaming.Lawyer.

Mitch can often be seen on several livestreaming platforms giving legal tips or business advice, interviewing fascinating guests, showing behind-the-scenes footage at the office, speaking from the stage, and sharing beautiful views of the California beach on his morning runs. In addition, after seeing so many people dangerously livestream while driving, Mitch also started a movement to raise awareness of the dangers of livestreaming while driving via http://StopDD.today and using #StopDD.

I asked Mitch if he could share his best advice for other professionals who are interested in using livestreaming to build their brand and expand their top-of-mind awareness from local to global. Here is what he shared:

Jennifer Quinn

"Be prepared, add value through your expertise, show your human side, and always engage with your audience. Give yourself permission to be real and be yourself."

In Mitch's opinion, these are the keys to success when it comes to professionals interested in livestreaming.

6. Companies Wanting to Attract Quality Employees

Job hunting has changed dramatically with the inception of the internet, and the game just changed again with the increased consumption of video. As a company, nothing is more valuable than quality employees. You are only as strong as your weakest link. And, once you bring on a new-hire, you invest in onboarding and training. Doesn't it make sense to do all that you can before that to make sure the new employee is a good match for your company?

Livestreaming is a great way to highlight your company culture and mission. Using live video on your social media platforms shows perspective employees what they can expect. Depending on how you use it, they might even get to meet future co-workers before they ever set foot in the office!

Also, if your company wants to attract millennials, livestreaming conveys the authenticity that they value.

Chapter 4:
Building Authority Using Livestreaming

The most common way to build authority and demonstrate expertise has been to publish a book. Many professionals look at authoring expertise books as an expanded business card. It makes sense. However, there are a lot of resources that are needed to publish a book: time, money, know-how, connections, etc.

Creating live video is virtually in everyone's pocket with the advanced technology of smartphones. Opening an app and hitting "Go Live" gives every person an equal opportunity to establish authority.

In her latest book, *How to Become the Most Published Expert in Your Industry: Publishing is Way Bigger Than a Book*, Terilee Harrison teaches that building your authority is all about consistently publishing online content. This includes livestreaming, podcasting, videos, and publishing articles on LinkedIn.

I asked Terilee what her thoughts were specifically on how businesses and brands could optimize livestreaming to build authority. Here is her response:

"Every business person needs to build their authority- whether you are a professional in the corporate world, a business owner, or an independent contractor for a larger company. These are the benefits you can expect to receive by building your authority by incorporating livestreaming:

- *People perceive you to be smarter*
- *You become known as a thought leader*
- *Clients beg to work with you*
- *You have a rapidly growing email list and social media following*
- *You gain increased clarity about your message and movement*
- *You have opportunities to speak in front of large audiences*
- *Business owners look to you for partnerships*
- *You build a meaningful legacy and a way to make a difference now*

Do you want these results? It's time to begin livestreaming. Livestreaming is one of the best ways to build your authority! You create an energy around you when you consistently livestream. People begin to follow you saying, "Wow! He or she is everywhere! Look at what he or she is doing." People will want to do business with you.

The key to building your authority as an expert is consistency. I believe in the power of livestreaming so much that I've started doing it myself. I recall enthusiastically telling JennyQ I was going to begin livestreaming three times a week to start! She brought me back to reality and suggested I begin by consistently going live one time a week. Start by building the habit. Become more confident. Begin to build my audience. She was right! It is better to start with a goal you can reach, and build from there, rather than to overcommit and under-deliver.

Imagine with me for a minute how building your authority through livestreaming might benefit your business. As an example, what if you were the most published mortgage lender in your city? If you livestream consistently, even at the rate of just once a week to start, you will publish 50+ livestreams over the course of a year.

- *There are potential clients looking for a lender...*
- *Your past clients need to refinance...*
- *Realtors are looking for mortgage professionals to partner with...*

If any of these people find you online and compare you to another mortgage professional they were also referred to, who has not been consistently publishing online content, who do you think would have the advantage of being hired? You would! You are an expert in your field! Do you think that would impact your business?

One of the most effective ways to build authority is to speak about your target market's pain points. The more you speak and write about how you can solve what pains them, the more potential clients will be drawn to you.

For example, I work with authors who want to establish themselves as an expert or share a message with the world. Some of the things that hold them back from reaching their writing goals are fear, procrastination, and time management. If I continue to speak on how I can help them push through what's holding them back, they will come back again and again to listen to my message. How can this work for you in your industry? If you aren't sure what your target market's pain points are, ask them. For example, you can create a poll on Facebook. They will tell you!

Another important aspect of building your authority is social currency. When your livestreaming strategy includes interviewing other experts, you build social currency with other professionals. Social currency is when people share things that make them look good to others. Social currency is something you give to someone, and there's just something about it- it's not that you expect they're going to give something back to you, but if you've given to them, it's more likely that they might.

Livestreaming is an incredible way to meet and connect with people from all over the world, because you're always looking for someone to be a guest on your show. People love the opportunity to promote their business as a guest, and you build social currency."

Chapter 5:
Which Platform Should I Livestream From?

This might be the most common question I get from new livestreamers. The answer, albeit frustrating, is, "It depends."

- It depends on what your overall marketing strategy is
- It depends on where your target demographic is hanging out
- It depends on where your existing audience is
- It depends on how many followers/subscribers you have on certain platforms
- It depends on how much time you have to devote to your livestreaming efforts

The good news is that the skills acquired in livestreaming on ANY platform transfer to livestreaming on ALL platforms. That being said, the most important thing is to choose one and get started.

For building a business and brand, the most used and viewed live video platforms are:
1. Facebook Live
2. YouTube Live
3. Twitter/Periscope
4. Instagram

Looking over the list, ask yourself the easiest question to answer:

Which platform does my business or brand already have the most engagement and/or the most followers? That answer will more than likely give you the best starting point where to start livestreaming. But, it's important to measure both the follower count AND the current engagement.

CASE STUDY

Let's look below at the example of Jan Smith, Realtor. Jan wants to start implementing livestreaming into her marketing strategy by going live and showing properties using her smartphone, but does not know which platform to begin with. Here's her current social media standing:

- *Facebook business page – 1,500 followers*
- *YouTube channel – 40 subscribers*

- *Twitter – 15,000 followers*
- *Instagram – 250 followers*

At first glance, here's what we know:

1. *YouTube is not an option for Jan because livestreaming from a mobile device is not currently offered with so few subscribers.*
2. *Jan has the most followers in Twitter, which is good for livestreaming from either Periscope or Twitter because of their relationship. Periscope livestreams autoplay in tweets.*

Taking a closer look, however, we find the following:

1. *Engagement on Twitter is relatively low on impressions, retweets, and "favorites."*
2. *Facebook has a high level of engagement with posts getting comments, likes, and shares.*
3. *Instagram has a moderate level of engagement.*

You can see how even though Twitter has the most followers, Facebook seems to make the most sense for Jan to use for her livestreaming. In addition to it being a great place for Jan to increase her current visibility, another factor that plays into this is that Jan can use targeted Facebook ads to drive traffic to her live videos afterwards.

Regardless of which platform you choose to go live from, there are some tried and true livestreaming best practices that translate to each platform. These are covered in **Section 2: Broadcasting Basics.**

SECTION 2:
BROADCASTING BASICS

Jenny ⬛Live.com

Chapter 6:
Gear and Equipment

There are three main areas to pay attention to when getting started with livestreaming. The great news is, you probably already have them all! I've made recommendations in this chapter, but if you want a super easy clickable link, please go to http://Gear.JennyQ.Live and I will immediately send you an email with links to all the equipment I talk about here.

These three main equipment areas are:

- Video
- Audio
- Lighting

1. Beginner - Must-Have to Get Started

Video - Beginner

To record your video, you will need a webcam or a mobile device. Most computers have a built-in webcam that has decent quality. Smartphones and tablets have cameras that are utilizing some relatively advanced video technology as well.

As you are just beginning, it is completely reasonable to start with what you have. If you are going to be livestreaming from different locations, it makes sense to use your mobile device for broadcasting.

To improve the video and how you look on screen you'll want to ensure that you have a very stable video feed. There are two ways to accomplish this:

1. Make sure you have the bandwidth necessary to livestream without having your video being pixelated or having your live feed ended for poor signal. If you're broadcasting from your computer, the best option is to be hardwired to an ethernet connection. If a hard connection is not possible, or if you are broadcasting from your mobile device, check the strength of your connection by running a test of

upload and download speed. Simply go to a testing site (Google "Internet speed test") or download a speed test app from iTunes or the Google Play Store. This step will save you a lot of headache and/or embarrassment!

2. When livestreaming began, viewers were much more tolerant of wobbly video, but no more. You will want to buy a tripod or other stabilizing mount to position your smartphone or tablet.
Regardless of the mount you choose, make sure you keep your device stable so that it's not shaky or wobbly. Unstable video streams lose viewers fast.

Audio - Beginner

I can't underscore the importance of audio in your livestreams enough. But to try, I want to share what Ross Brand, founder of http://LivestreamUniverse.com and on-air broadcaster, shared when I asked him "What's the most important thing for new livestreamers to pay attention to?"

"The most important aspect of your live video is...audio. Why? Because for most livestream content, the key to your broadcast is what you have to say when talking about your topic of the day and your business. Your voice

is the primary mode of communicating with your audience, whether informing or entertaining them. You can listen without the video and still enjoy the talk show, but if the audio is choppy or failing, how long will people stay tuned trying to read your lips?

Thus, audio quality is the first thing you should look to improve and optimize when starting out or advancing as a livestreamer. It doesn't have to cost a lot, but make sure you have, at minimum, ear buds or headphones and some type of microphone that is better than the one built into your computer or webcam.

Even the mic on your iPhone or Android ear buds is better than going with the built-in mic on your computer or webcam."

Lighting - Beginner

Chances are you probably don't pay much attention to lighting when it comes to taking pictures or being on camera. It took me doing a lot of live video broadcasts for me to realize that everything about the livestream is better with quality lighting. From the viewer experience to how I actually look on screen, lighting makes a big difference!

Good news! The best lighting is also FREE lighting! Daylight is the best lighting you can have. To best utilize it, sit in front of a window, facing the window, with your device in front of you. Take care that the device is not casting a shadow on your face. Also, note if the lighting is so bright that it washes you out. If that's the case, simply draw the curtain or sheer to act as a diffuser.

If you're broadcasting at a time when there is not daylight, there's a simple and inexpensive solution: You can buy a ring light that attaches to your mobile device or laptop. You can buy one for under $20 on Amazon or from Arkon Mounts.

Good lighting will set you apart from amateur livestreamers. It creates instant credibility if you are well lit and not broadcasting from what looks like your mother's basement. If for no other reason, pay attention to the lighting because it takes years off your age!

2. Intermediate – Investing in Equipment

If you are broadcasting to build your brand, you will want to present yourself in a professional and credible way to instantly convey authority, right? Some of these subtle nuances can make or break the viewer's perception of your credibility. You have 8-10 seconds to make an impression, and these are some ways you can take away some possible negative dings to your authority.

Let's have a quick review of what it would take to put together a nice home/office studio for a small investment.

Video - Intermediate

If you are using a mobile device, invest under $100 to get an olloclip® lens clip or something similar. This allows you to have wide-angle shots, micro shots, and fish-eye shots. It will really set you apart from other livestreamers who typically use their device camera and sit directly in front of the camera, looking like a talking head.

For desktop video, invest in an external webcam designed for livestreaming. A good entry-level USB webcam is the Logitech® C922 ProCam for around $100 on Amazon. New technology is coming out all the time, so it's worth it to do a little research before buying.

Audio - Intermediate

Again, looking to Ross Brand, founder of LivestreamUniverse.com, for his thoughts, he gives his advice for a professional approach to audio in the home/office studio:

"If you can, get a good entry-level broadcast dynamic microphone in the $50-80 range for when you are using your desktop or laptop computer. A few of the more popular microphones in that price range come with a USB connection so you can plug it directly into the computer as well as an XLR connection for plugging it into a mixer or audio interface. As you start out, you will likely be using the mic's USB cable.

You will notice a significant improvement in how you sound using one of these entry-level broadcast mics. Go for a dynamic mic rather than a condenser mic, as condensers pick up too much background noise. You also want to make sure to get an inexpensive boom arm so that your mic isn't sitting on your desk or table (picking up keyboard noise and forcing you to sit hunched over for extended periods), and a foam windscreen, which will help block out noise from your breathing. For entry-level broadcast mics, you shouldn't need to spend more than $20 on a functional boom arm and foam windscreen."

Jennifer Quinn

Great advice from Ross. Many livestreaming broadcasters have had great results using the Audio-Technica® ATR2100 USB mic which sells for around $80 on Amazon.

Lighting - Intermediate

Studio lighting can be a bit cumbersome, but it's worth it. The value that good lighting adds to the quality of your livestreams and credibility of your authority is worth the expense and trouble.

Ideally, you'll want a 3-point box lighting system. Position them so that two of the lights are in front of you, one off to the right and the other off to the left. The third one is positioned behind you and overhead, offering back lighting.

The box lighting kit I use is Fancierstudio® 2000 Watt Lighting Kit – photo studio lighting with two 16"x24" softbox lights and one 16"x16" softbox for hair light, and it sells for around $150 on Amazon. (The term "softbox" refers to a collapsible fabric reflector that the light is mounted in.)

Another lighting kit I use for powerful mobile lighting is the Neewer® 2x160 LED Dimmable Ultra High Power

Panel Lighting Kit for Digital Camera Camcorder. This is also sold on Amazon for around $150. This is great for a portable option, but it requires keeping batteries charged; therefore, I recommend you buy an extra charger and set of batteries.

Chapter 7:
Basic Skills for Livestreaming

So far in this book we've talked about who should be livestreaming and why. We've covered the gear and equipment needs, and also talked about what to expect on your first broadcast. We've talked about which platform you should begin livestreaming from and why the timing to start livestreaming is now.

There are a few basic skills you can learn that, once mastered, will put your livestreams into a different league than all other beginning livestreamers (and many experienced ones!).

There is an art to livestreaming, which comes in the nuances that are so subtle many people miss them. That's what we're going to talk about now. The nuances.

Jennifer Quinn

The subtleties. The things that make you gain instant trust and credibility with your viewers. Remember, the purpose of livestreaming is to build relationships by increasing the know, like and trust factor. With that in mind, let's cover some of the basic things you can do to show up as people expect you to.

1. Looking into the Camera Lens

Why is this so hard? Well, because it's awkward. Unless you've had training in television or broadcasting, looking into the lens of a camera is not really a skill most of us have ever considered before.

When you are livestreaming, whether you are using your desktop or a mobile device, you see your own face staring back at you.

The only other time we see our face is when we are looking into a mirror. Typically, we look into the mirror when we are assessing ourselves to see if we look presentable.

Now, suddenly, we are on a screen looking at our own faces, and habit dictates that we continuously assess how we look. The added variable is that we are talking, moving, and animating ourselves. We are not used to seeing ourselves like this. So, we keep looking. And looking. And looking.

The typical livestreamer bounces between reading the on-screen comments and looking at their own face. This creates a distance between the viewer and the broadcaster, because at no time is the broadcaster ever looking "at" the viewer. It's subtle, but in this scenario, the broadcaster is being observed by the viewer, not engaging with the viewer.

When the broadcaster makes the small shift of looking into the camera lens, no matter how awkward it feels, suddenly the viewer *feels connected* to the broadcaster because of the eye contact, and a very basic human need is satisfied.

It's not practical, or even possible, for a broadcaster on livestreaming to maintain digital eye contact with the viewer 100% of the time, but if it can be done 70-80% of the time, the feeling of connection is there, and the opportunity to build the know, like, and trust factor is much greater.

Jennifer Quinn

Tricks to Master Looking into the Camera Lens

If you have difficulty with this, you are definitely not alone. The first time I realized how vital it was to look at the lens of the camera, I was doing daily interviews on "The Daily Q Show" on Blab. The feedback that I got from viewers is that I needed to look at the camera more because it seemed like I was looking down, around, and not paying attention. The reality was that I was looking at, and was fully engaged with, my guest. However, to both the viewers and my guest, it felt like I was not paying attention to them.

So, I started experimenting with looking directly into the lens of the webcam, even while my guest was talking. Doing so *felt* inauthentic to me. It *felt* like I was ignoring the guest I had on my show. But what actually happened is that everyone felt more connected to me. People perceived me as caring more and being present.

This is not an easy habit to master, but here are a few tricks that I've used and picked up along the way:
1. Picture your guest's image inside the camera lens
2. Picture one of your favorite people on the other side of the camera lens and that you are talking to them

3. Put a picture of loved ones above your webcam, or even cut a hole in a picture and tape it so you see your camera lens through the hole

4. Affix craft-store googly eyes to the camera lens

5. Write a note saying, "Look here!" and tape next to camera

6. Imagine your ideal client (avatar) on the other side of the camera lens and speak directly to them

A note about locating your camera lens on your mobile device:

Practice this before going live by opening your camera app, switch it to front facing (with your face on the screen), and locate the lens. If you're having difficulty doing this, one way is to move your finger around until you see it "block the shot" or show up on your screen. The lens is where your finger is!

Now, before you go live, practice looking at the lens and talking. Look back and forth (as if you're looking at comments on the screen) from the lens to the screen so that you can commit the location of the camera to memory.

You will feel silly doing this. Do it anyway. It's worth it.

2. Phone Orientation (holding your phone the right direction)

When you're livestreaming from your smartphone, there are two different orientations: portrait and landscape. Portrait orientation is when the device is vertical, or taller than it is wide. Landscape orientation is when the device is horizontal, or wider than it is tall.

This seems like a small detail, but the reason it matters is because each platform has an orientation that presents better to the viewers.

Perhaps you've seen someone go live on Facebook (a platform that prefers landscape orientation) with portrait orientation: the video appears with the broadcaster in the middle and a blurred greyish area on both sides of the frame. The blurry area comprises about half of the available screen space and forces the viewer to see a very limited shot of your broadcast.

You will notice the same thing with YouTube. The whole platform is based on landscape orientation. Instagram, on the other hand, heavily prefers portrait orientation for its live videos.

Periscope is "bilingual" when it comes to phone orientation, because the view switches inside the app itself depending on both the broadcaster's and viewer's phone position. It's interesting to note that with Periscope broadcasts now being viewable on Apple TV, the current preferred orientation for the best visual experience is landscape orientation.

With virtual reality and 360-degree views becoming more of an active component of livestreaming, the preferred phone direction will largely be landscape orientation.

3. Engagement with Viewers

The thing that sets live video apart from on-demand video is the ability for you to engage with your viewer in real time, and an opportunity for them to engage with you. Personal connection happens during a live broadcast, and profound personal connection happens when the broadcaster is also skilled at engaging.

As with any new skill, engaging with your viewers is going to take practice, and lots of it.

One thing I tell my coaching clients is this – If you don't want to engage with your viewers in real-time, then don't do livestreaming. On-demand videos are still very much an effective marketing tool and offer different benefits than livestreaming, one of them being that you are able to edit them before sharing. This fits very well for many people's time availability, temperament, and marketing strategy. For this very reason, I co-created a Video Marketing Jumpstart course. (see Resources)

One thing livestreaming offers over on-demand video is the real-time connection and an opportunity for the viewer to spontaneously participate in the broadcast. Remember this basic truth about human beings and your livestreams will be magical: *People want to be seen, recognized, and validated.* When you are able to meet that need on your livestreams, you've made real human connection, even when you can't see your viewers.

So, how do you make that livestreaming magic happen? Here are some basic skills you can start implementing with your broadcasts:

1. *Eye contact with viewers* – look into the lens of the camera 70-80% of the broadcast

2. *Bring viewers into your world* – be vulnerable and real. Share personal stories and anecdotes. Give them a glimpse of your world.

3. *Explain things* and create context for what is happening live – For example, if there is a loud noise in the background, explain that your cat just knocked over the vase, rather than act like nothing happened. If you heard something, chances are your viewers did too.

4. *Don't assume they know what you know* – in other words, over communicate, over explain, over demonstrate. You never know who is watching your live broadcast or your replay.

5. *Do not wait for people to join the broadcast* – immediately start into your content instead of waiting for a certain number of viewers to join. A good rule of thumb is to say a quick hello to the live viewers *and the replay viewers*, then move into the content you are there to deliver. A big error that people make here is that they wait to start their content until they have X number of people. It's not respectful to the viewer who jumped onto your livestream when you began, nor will it keep the replay viewer engaged and willing to stick around until you get to your content.

6. *Welcome people by name* – People love to hear their name, and what better way to make someone feel

seen, recognized, and validated, than to welcome them to the broadcast by name! This isn't always possible to do, however. Generally speaking, without diluting your content, every chance you get give a quick shout out to people by name, as if they just joined your party already in progress.

7. *Avoid private jokes* – unless you bring the audience in on the joke. It's tempting to say a quick private joke to a friend or colleague who hops on to your broadcast, but if you leave it standing as a private joke then you've just alienated the rest of your viewers. If you do want to go there with a private joke, then circle back around with an explanation of the joke so that everyone can have a laugh and feel like they are a part of the "inner circle."

Remember, people *want* to connect with you, be recognized, and be seen! They want to learn from you, they want to buy from you, but they won't be able to do either of those if they don't feel validated. When they can resonate with you—your energy, your vulnerability, your approachability—then they will connect with you, and they will be able to trust you to open their minds to learn, and open their pocketbooks to buy.

4. What to Expect on Your First Broadcast

What would you say if I were to ask you, "What is the number one reason people give for not using live video in their marketing strategy?"

If you guessed FEAR, then you are correct! People are afraid of doing it wrong, looking stupid, not knowing what to say, and making mistakes. If you feel that way as well, then you're in good company! We all felt that way before we went live on video.

When I started on Periscope it would take me a full 30 minutes to prepare for a three-minute broadcast. I was so nervous that I was sweaty and shaking! I wanted to make sure I was doing it right and that I wouldn't make a fool of myself.

But then, I landed on one of Dave Shrein's Periscope broadcasts. He had been livestreaming a few months longer than I had, and he gave this wise advice: "Your first 100 broadcasts are going to suck, so just know that, get through them, and learn as you go!"

For me, that was liberating! It gave me permission to let go of my perfectionist tendencies and just focus on getting through my first 100 broadcasts!

Side note: I actually reached my 100th broadcast while I was in New York City at the first Periscope Summit in September 2015, attended by over 500 international livestreamers. Dave Shrein was there and he graciously agreed to be on my 100th Periscope broadcast with me as we went live from the summit!

Now, back to YOUR first broadcasts and that pesky thing called FEAR. I have a few tips and tricks that I wish I would have known at the beginning that will help you alleviate the fear. (Reality check: I said alleviate not eradicate. It's okay to feel fear. You can still do it! As long as you have 1% more of something else than fear, you're golden! 49% Fear / 51% Motivation – you're in!)

1. Before you even go live on any platform, the best way to learn is to watch other people's livestreams. You want to watch a variety of different types of live video so you can see different styles. What I mean by that is that you should watch a variety of people who are livestreaming. Don't limit it just to people in your industry and what they are doing on live video broadcasts, but watch other industries and see what they are doing. You might find something that someone is doing that would translate very well to

your industry and/or audience. As you watch –
become a student!

- Take notes
- Ask yourself what you like, what you don't like
- How do they engage with the audience?
- How do they deliver their message?
- How do they conduct interviews?
- How is their lighting, their background, their audio, etc…
- And as a viewer- ENGAGE with the broadcaster and the other viewers by using live comments during the livestream! You'll find you can organically build your following not only by livestreaming yourself, but by participating in others' livestreams as well.

2. Prepare what you're going to say. Here's a simple formula to format what you'll talk about.

    - Choose a topic you can easily talk about for 10 minutes. For your first broadcast, the chosen topic does not have to be in the area of your expertise or industry. You just want a topic that you know inside and out, up and down, backward and forwards. It can even be as simple as the most effective way to fold laundry or how to mow a lawn!

- On a sticky note write down your introduction, three bulleted talking points, and your exit or outro:
    i. Intro can be as simple as, "Hi, I'm JennyQ and I'm going to tell you the secrets to having livestreams that convert to sales!"
    ii. Bullets
        1. Talking point 1
        2. Talking point 2
        3. Talking point 3
    iii. Exit or outro can be a Call-to-Action, such as, "If you found this valuable, please share it!" or you can say your favorite quote, "I just want to end by sharing my favorite quote, 'When someone hands you the tools of success, embrace them with enthusiasm!'"
- Place sticky note in front of you – either on the monitor of the computer or on your mobile device. If this seems like it's in the way, go ahead and hold the sticky note or have it on the table. It's okay to glance down at it to have a reminder of what's next.

3. Practice in private. Most livestreaming platforms have the option to adjust privacy settings so that you can control who sees the livestream broadcast. Some

of them even allow you to set the setting to "only me." Alternatively, you can practice by simply using the video recorder on your device.

You're feeling better already, aren't you? :)

4. Watch the replay and take notes. This is tricky because as of yet I have not met anyone who likes to watch their video replay or listen to their recorded voice. But this is an important step. This is a huge learning opportunity for you to get really great at livestreaming. When you watch your replays, make it a habit to do these few things:

- Be kind to yourself. As I said, no one likes to see themselves on video. You will see things that you had no idea you did because we never see ourselves in action. I suspect you'll dislike about 80% of what you see. That's okay! You will have an opportunity to change or adjust those things if you choose to! But here's the good news: there will be about 20% of the things that you do that you will like! You might even say, "Oh! I didn't know I did that! That's cool!!"

- Ask yourself these two questions when watching your replay. The wording is important, because they will yield answers that are useful and not merely critical. The questions are:

- What went well?
- What could have gone better?
- If you do catch yourself being critical, simply flip it into something like, "Oh! I'm glad I saw that! Now I can adjust the lighting next time so there's not a shadow on my face!"

5. Content Ideas

It's truly a toss-up as to which question I am asked the most as a livestreaming consultant, but "What do I talk about?" is definitely one of the top, and it's usually phrased with some colorful language and/or expletives.

The frustration of not knowing what to talk about is not really about not having knowledge to share; it is more about being afraid of making a fool of yourself if you don't do it "right."

Everyone has something they know enough about to talk about for 10 minutes. In fact, when most people step into their area of passion or expertise, it is normally hard to get them to stop! So, the question then becomes, how can you find different ways to creatively share your knowledge with people that will be compelling and add value?

When deciding what type of content to create using livestreaming as part of your overall marketing strategy, it's important to keep a few things in mind:

- What is your overall marketing strategy?
- What do you want to accomplish with live video?

The answers to those questions will drive the direction you should take with the content of your livestream broadcasts.

You want to make sure that your content is both aligned with your business while also providing viewers value in the way of entertainment, education, inspiration, fun, or information.

Here are 10 content ideas that can be modified for almost any industry, business or brand:

1. Behind the scenes - show how things work - process, system, etc..
   o What is common and everyday to you is probably very interesting to your viewers. Did you ever watch Mr. Roger's Neighborhood as a child? Weren't the field trips the best part? What do you have in your life or business that could be a virtual field trip for your viewers?

2. Q & A – #AMA
   o Q & A stands for "Questions and Answers" and #AMA stands for "Ask Me Anything." Both of which essentially have the same concept. Jump on a live broadcast and open it up for viewers to ask you questions about yourself and/or your business. You set the guidelines by which questions you answer. Be prepared in the event that you don't immediately have viewers, or your viewers don't have questions. In this case, I would solicit questions from people you know ahead of time so that you can read them and answer on your livestream during the inevitable "lull" on your Q & A broadcast.

3. Educational / How To
   o Arguably one of the most popular topics for all content, not just live video! People love to learn! Teach a specific way to do something or a new skill that not everyone has.

4. Interviews
   o While you certainly can do formal interviews, don't rule out the casual interview with co-workers, employees, man on the street, best friend, hair dresser, etc... You get the idea.

5. What are the questions people ask you regularly?
    o   In every industry there are 10 questions that people are asked most often. Write those down. Now you have 10 ideas for livestream broadcasts. Pro tip: Keep a running list of questions people ask you.

6. Newsjacking
    o   Newsjacking is where you insert your unique business perspective into a breaking news story and do a livestream broadcast about it. Use caution when doing so, though, because you don't want to exploit disasters or violence to promote your business or brand.

7. Behind the Scenes / Sneak Peek
    o   For example, if you are about to go on stage, do a book signing, attend a conference, or do a workshop, you can go live and show the preparation that goes into it. This is not limited to the day of the event. If you are prepping for a keynote speech, you can go live to talk about the content of the talk, show the slide deck, or take people with you shopping to buy the outfit you will wear during the keynote address.

8. Rant
   - A rant is exactly what it says! You go on livestream to rant about something. Always be mindful of how this aligns with your brand and represents your business.

9. Recycle existing content from previous writing, blogs, vlogs, videos, etc..
   - Perhaps the easiest way to get content for your livestream is to breathe new life into old content. Take a video from YouTube that you did two years ago, update any relevant information, then go live! Likewise, you can take an old blog post with evergreen content from ten years ago and use that as a topic for livestreaming.

10. Live events – capture footage – at a conference, grab a speaker for a quick interview or a musician for a back-stage interview.
    - People love to be where the action is! If you are at a conference or concert, don't be shy. Ask someone that your viewers would find interesting for a quick interview! They might say no, but they might say yes!

Chapter 8:
Fear and The Plan to Overcome It

One thing that never surprises me is the variety of ways that people can disguise their fear about going live. I don't blame them, though. It IS scary. So is starting a new job on the first day. Or asking someone out on a date. Or going to the doctor to get test results. Our lives are filled with things that push us out of our comfort zones. Unless you have been able to create a life where you sit home, have food delivered, never interact with other humans, and shield yourself from all news and happenings around the world, it's a safe bet to say that you overcome fear on a regular basis. It is part of being human: being afraid, developing courage, overcoming, and ultimately succeeding.

I'm often impressed with the creativity people have when I hear their "reasons" for convincing themselves that livestreaming would never work for them. Here are a few:

I'm afraid to look stupid.

What if I do it wrong?

People will judge me.

I don't have enough time.

What about the trolls?

How do I know what to say?

I have a face for radio.

What if something goes wrong?

I don't know my platform.

No one cares what I have to say.

I don't want people to steal my ideas.

It's too much to learn.

It's a fad.

I don't know whom I would broadcast to.

I'm a private person.

I don't want to make a fool of myself.

My industry is boring.

What's the point?

No one would watch me on video.

My opinions are too strong; I'll scare people away!

Too many people might see me.

I'd be embarrassed if – my parents / children / boss / someone I know / someone I don't know - watched this.

How did that feel reading the list of reasons people give for not going live? Did you identify with any of them? Did you feel compassion for some of the reasons, thinking, "Oh! I could totally see how someone could feel that way!"

The reality is, none of these are true. They are simply stories we tell ourselves, somehow intended to protect us from taking action, moving forward, and possibly even succeeding. It reminds me of a story I once heard:

Once upon a time there was a farmer who lived with his wife in their farmhouse. Their nearest neighbor was miles away and the farmer liked it that way. He really enjoyed his time alone and being with just his wife and his animals.

One day there was a knock at the door. The farmer's wife answered the door and saw one of their distant neighbors standing there.

"Hi! May I help you?" asked the farmer's wife.

"I was wondering if I could borrow your axe. My handle broke, the stores are closed, and I need to finish chopping wood before the sun sets," replied the neighbor.

"Oh, hold on please. Let me get my husband," said the farmer's wife.

The farmer came to the door and looked his neighbor up and down. The farmer's wife stood by his side as he said to the neighbor, "May I help you?"

The neighbor replied, "I was wondering if I could borrow your axe. My handle broke, the stores are closed, and I need to finish chopping wood before the sun sets."

The farmer thought for a minute.

He looked at his neighbor, and said, "No. I'm sorry I can't loan the axe to you, I'm making soup tonight."

Perplexed, the neighbor said, "I'm sorry to have bothered you, have nice evening."

After the farmer closed the door, his wife asked, "What did making soup have to do with you not loaning the axe to the neighbor?"

The farmer replied, "Any excuse will do!"

And so it is with anything in life. If you really want to do it, you'll find a way. If you really don't, you'll find an excuse.

If you're willing, I'd like for you to take a moment now and look back at the list of reasons people give for not wanting to start livestreaming. Imagine asking everyone you see why they aren't livestreaming to build their brand, and each person gives you one of those answers. Now, picture yourself responding with, "Any excuse will do!"

What was that imagining experience like? How was it different than the first time you read the list of reasons? Did you have more objectivity? Were you able to see how they really could simply be excuses for not wanting to get past the fear of trying something new?

There's a difference between using something as an excuse to avoid doing something, and stating a fear but being open to a way to overcome that fear. Below I discuss some of the reasons people have given, and the ways that I've helped them see that there is a solution, if they're willing to take it!

"I don't have enough time"

When I hear this, what I hear is "I don't yet see the value to make it worthwhile for me to make livestreaming a consistent part of my marketing strategy." What WOULD it take for you to make it worth your while to make time to livestream?

- Is there a specific amount of money you would want to make to show you a return on your investment?
- Are you interested in social proof? Meaning- you will have a certain number of views, comments, and engagement on your livestreams?
- Would changing people's lives in a real and meaningful way make it worth your while? What kinds of changes?
- Would it be making connections with people from around the world?
- What would you have to see, hear, receive, feel, or think in order to know that making this broadcast was worth your while?

Getting very clear on what YOU would need to see as a result of livestreaming, and having a clear plan to achieve it, would make it far more worth your while to make the time to fit livestreaming into your marketing strategy than simply doing it because the research shows that live video content is now king. This clarity will also help guide you with what content to share, how to share it, and what audience to share it with.

"I'm an introvert"

I find it interesting that introverts and extroverts experience livestreaming differently, yet both groups benefit greatly from it! The livestreaming community doesn't seem to be weighted more towards either group. In my experience, livestreaming is a way for both types of people to get their message out to the world and use their unique abilities to connect with their audience.

One of the big differences is that extroverts are typically energized by livestreaming while introverts generally need to plan time to recharge post-broadcast.

For example, an introvert might need to have more preparation, finely tuned content, a quiet space to broadcast from, and scheduled downtime to recharge after the livestream ends. Having a clear plan can alleviate a lot of the stress of going live, especially for introverts! Some of the most successful and popular livestreamers are introverts, so don't let anyone tell you that you can't be a livestreamer!

Recently we discussed introverts and livestreaming in my "Go Live! Insiders Community" private Facebook group and here's what one successful, self-proclaimed "extroverted introvert" livestreamer said:

"As an extroverted introvert, I thrive on the connections with viewers, guests, co-hosts, and people commenting in the chat during and after the show. But one of my biggest challenges is that I find even short livestreams require recovery time.

Speaking takes energy, and speaking publicly or to others socially and professionally does contribute to emptying the tank for introverts. However, because introverts are internally focused, they do tend to have focused presentations that can be very effective, as they know well what they are trying to accomplish."

"People will judge me"

Recently I gave a presentation on livestreaming and received the following comment from an attendee.

She raised her hand and said, "When I'm on Facebook and I see livestreams coming across my newsfeed I think to myself, 'I don't care what people are saying on their livestreams!' How do I use livestreaming for my business and not have people scroll past mine thinking, 'I don't care!'"

As I dug more deeply into her question, I realized it was two-fold.

> #1 - She wanted to know how to make her content powerful and strong so that people did care!
>
> #2 - She was afraid that people would judge her.

Valid points! And simple solutions to both.

Being afraid that people will judge you is a normal part of life. People judge us everywhere we go. Livestreaming is no different.

The trick is to become so confident in the message you're sharing during the broadcast that you realize you aren't doing it for the haters; you're doing it for the people who need to hear what you have to say!

Going Live ISN'T ABOUT YOU

More often than not, the reason we feel fear is because we buy into the belief that our livestream is about us. Admittedly, when you're on live video, it FEELS like everything is about you. After all, it's your face on camera, your name and image on the promotional graphic, your voice that people are listening to, etc.

But, unless you're only on livestreaming to get attention, your live broadcast is about the viewer. Whether you're helping a future customer with your product, a future client with your service, or an audience member with your story, your livestream is about THEM and not YOU.

When I was in school I was a choir geek. There. I said it. But it's true. I often performed in musicals. My 'claim to fame' is that at age 14 I was cast in Boise State University's "Sound of Music" as Liesl.

To say I was nervous would be an understatement! I was terrified! I was so afraid of making a mistake or doing it wrong! It didn't help that when we had our first full dress rehearsal with the orchestra I completely blew it. The actor who played Rolfe, Liesl's love interest, and I forgot our choreography.

Do you remember the scene where Rolfe and Liesl sneak out to the gazebo and share a song and a dance ending with a kiss? It was that scene where we completely forgot our dance, missed our cues, and stood frozen on stage. There we were, with our director watching, as we stood helpless not knowing what to do. The director was the stereotypical staunch, stuffy, and strict professor. He was not amused.

The music sounded so different to us with a full orchestra versus the recorded soundtrack we had been practicing with. We didn't want to make a fool of ourselves, so we kept trying desperately to recover, failing at every turn. Well, we did pick up one musical cue- the kiss at the end, which, in and of itself, is an embarrassing fact to admit.

Regardless, what came from it has been a lifelong lesson for me, and it applies to livestreaming so well. Afterward, I shared with an actor who had more experience than me in theater how it was so awful and how fear got the best of me!

She replied with, "The reason you are nervous and feel fear is because you are worried about what people will think of you. It's not about you. It's about the gifts you are sharing with the audience. It's about what you are GIVING to them. Focus on sharing your gift."

And so, I submit, going live ISN'T ABOUT YOU. It's about your viewers. It's about sharing your knowledge, gifts, passions, expertise, products, services, and ADDING VALUE to people's lives! When you take the FOCUS OFF YOURSELF and FOCUS ON THE VIEWERS, that's where the MAGIC HAPPENS!

Now, don't get me wrong - it's not THAT SIMPLE, is it? I mean, livestreaming is a new technology and having a plan cannot be underestimated. I will talk about my V.A.M. Video Success Plan in the next chapter, but to wrap this one up, remember this: Your fear, even though it feels so real, is probably an excuse. When you focus on what you're GIVING instead of the excuses, that's when you will make livestreaming magic happen!

Chapter 9:

V.A.M. Video Success Plan

Having participated in and watched thousands of livestreams, I've narrowed the primary keys to livestreaming success down to three specific areas. When I coach one-on-one clients, we develop a plan specific to their audience in these areas. There really are no shortcuts to live video success. If you don't nail each one of these three areas, then you will not achieve your livestreaming goals. Period.

It all comes down to this: **V.A.M.**

- **Viewers**
- **Authority**
- **Message**

If you don't have a plan for each one of these then you're not going to succeed in creating momentum, building awareness, and increasing business. This is the exact process I use when coaching one-on-one clients. We dive deep into creating and crafting each of these three areas.

1. Viewers

Your viewers are paramount. They can be live viewers or replay viewers, but you need to have viewers, otherwise your authority and message will be for nothing.

The first steps to getting viewers are to know five things: How to build your avatar; When to schedule the broadcasts; How to promote the broadcasts; When to start promoting; and Making sure your copy (description of your video) is crafted for your specific avatar.

An avatar is that ONE PERSON who perfectly represents the client you are looking for. For example, a realtor might have this avatar:

"My avatar is 34. Her name is Alaina, and she is a VP at a bank. She's been wanting to move out of her apartment to buy her first house, but she doesn't know where to start. She has good credit and a solid savings account, but she is unsure about home ownership and whether or not the timing is right

for her because she plans to travel a lot – plus, she's been dating her boyfriend for two years, but they are not engaged.

Alaina's parents live in the area and she loves to spend time with them. Alaina also enjoys entertaining her friends at her place and wants to start hosting out-of-state friends who want to visit. Alaina loves pets, and looks forward to having a yard so she can finally have a dog."

It is important to dial it in to the smallest detail on creating your avatar. Many people are hesitant to do this step because they feel that if they speak to one person in their marketing, they will lose so many other people. The truth is that it's actually the opposite: The more finely tuned your message is crafted, the more powerful it is, and the more people will be drawn to your message.

Once you have the avatar defined, you can make sure that everything in your marketing is directed toward that one person, including your livestreams, your graphics, and your promotions.

2. Authority

When a viewer hops on to your video, whether it's live or on replay, you have about 8-10 seconds to capture their attention. To do this, you need to pay attention to the details that create instant credibility and authority. Recall that what we are ultimately trying to do with livestreaming is to maximize the opportunity to build the know, like, and trust factor with people watching you.

The best way to build trust is to show up the way people expect to see you. Ask yourself, what does your avatar expect to see when they jump on your live video?

We can get all the viewers to your broadcast, but if they see a shaky camera, words appearing backwards on the screen, poor audio, shady lighting, or an incongruent background, people will not believe you and they will not stay to listen to your message.

It won't matter how good you are, how smart you are, how much you know, or how much you can change their life, those things need to be conveyed in such a way that your viewer feels that they trust you and your content from the moment you start your live broadcast.

It's like when you are at the doctor's office. If the doctor walks in and is wearing shorts, a tank top, flip flops, is holding a margarita and can't find his pen, his look and actions don't match his authority.

It's worth the time to pay attention to the small details so you don't trigger people (consciously or unconsciously) to question your authority within the first few seconds of hopping on your livestream.

3. Message

I truly believe that you can change the world one livestream at a time. I've experienced it myself, and I've watched it happen for others. And that's why your message is so important. Your message is going to change the world.

Your message might be a product or a service. It might be inspiration, motivation, support, or insight. Whatever your message is, make sure it's crafted specifically for your avatar.

Even if you are getting viewers, and your authority is evident, if your message isn't fine-tuned to your avatar, then you are spinning your wheels. As you begin livestreaming, you will be developing your style. As you do so, try different formats, take chances, and change things up, but all the while with your avatar in mind. What would SHE want to hear and see?

SUCCESS STORY: Glenn Dawson's V.A.M. Video Success Plan

Glenn Dawson is not just a personal trainer- he is MY personal trainer. In June 2016, I was hosting/emceeing a two-day event in Las Vegas. During the event, I met one of the attendees, Glenn Dawson, who is an online personal trainer.

One would be hard-pressed to think of an industry that is more saturated in the digital world than personal training. Glenn and I connected on Facebook, and when I returned home from the event I reached out to him to ask him a simple training question. After speaking with him, I realized that he had a different approach to training than I had ever heard.

In the previous year, I had lost 70 pounds using my own program, but I plateaued. I started working with Glenn, and within the next 12 months I overcame the plateau and lost another 84 pounds.

Now, that's all amazing, but what might be even more amazing is how Glenn has used live video to stand out from the crowd—the very crowded crowd of personal trainers—and catapulted his business using livestreaming. Not only this, he did it within a niche that many would have doubted that livestreaming would have any effectiveness at all.

Glenn Dawson has masterfully implemented the **V.A.M. Video Success Plan**. I asked him to share his story with us. While you're reading it, see if you can pick out where and how Glenn implemented the V.A.M. Video Success Plan!

No cash, no prospects, no hope

So, there I was, sitting alone on my guest room bed, door shut, my stomach turning itself into knots. Gravity felt heavier, pulling my whole body down. My lips quivered and my stomach sank, like right before you cry.

I faced the video camera, put on a fake smile and said, "Glenn Dawson here with Tools of Fitness, and I'm excited to have you guys on our webinar today to show you all how you can take these 'Five Steps to a Six pack!'"

Jennifer Quinn

This was a live webinar. Attended by ... only myself and my best friend / business partner, Brandon. We had to fake the whole webinar so we could have a chance to sell on the replay. This was our fourth webinar with no one attending, and my final hope for income. To make matters worse, I was down to my last $300, all that remained from when I left my corporate job to become an entrepreneur.

Brandon had also left his corporate job to join me in business, but shortly after putting in his notice (and consequently losing his insurance) he broke both his legs. All his remaining money went to surgery, and he had no other financial prospects.

More than anything, we needed to make money.

Switching up our game

We were lucky enough to go to a Mastermind in San Diego full of internet marketers to learn how to make the webinar work and finally make some money. Brandon and I drove there from Reno using our rent money. We sat through the Mastermind, furiously taking notes, looking for answers.

Towards the end of the Mastermind my friend and mentor Nehal had "the talk" with me, and began to lay out plans for a sales funnel. A GREAT sales funnel we could not afford.

Hearing this, he said, "How much money do you have? Like can you go to Starbucks and buy a coffee and not worry about it? Or are you getting the free water?"

Shamefully I told him "The water." I was at one of the lowest points in my life.

Nehal was such a good friend. He didn't need to do any of this, but he said, "We need to get you money first. When you are broke, you have a different mindset. I've been there. You think different. You make horrible decisions, and you constantly act like a starved dog looking for food."

That night he wrote out three pieces of paper, detailing how to put out a simple client application form, a website, and a change of our name and target market. We also went over a content plan that would cost no money, but would make us some.

For content, my first video was of my friend and mentor Tanner doing squats. Tanner was also my personal coaching client, and he used to have back pain. He wrote some good copy to accompany the video. I literally asked everyone I knew to share it. (In fact, for about a year, I would personally ask everyone I knew to share my posts.)

And then- I received a client application! I was so excited! This was my opportunity! I might actually have money!

I ended up getting six applications, and closed all of them. (These results are not typical. I used to train trainers how to sell, and closing sales is a special skill I've honed over the years.)

Each contract was between $567 and $2,000 per month, so needless to say, I gained a return on my first organic campaign with ZERO ad dollars spent.

But how would I get more clients?

I honestly didn't care, because even though I got personal coaching clients from the video, I was still convinced I was going to make our original webinar work, and I spent the next four months failing at it. I was such an idiot.

Then I was talking to another mentor (I have, like, nine mentors, and am super grateful for them). He asked why

I wasn't making $10,000 a month. I said, "The webinar isn't converting. We only had ten people on last time."

He then said something so simple and so easy I feel bad even writing about it. "You're a closer. Get people on the phone. Close them. It's that simple, Bro."

Wow. He was right. Then with the personal coaching money, I could spend money on everything else and really grow my business.

So instead of the webinar, I began to release case studies. Elaborate ones. And I started picking up coaching clients.

But after all that, I still only got to $8,000 a month. It was frustrating.

Finally – livestreaming is the answer

About a month later, at another Mastermind, I was telling the group how cortisol levels should only be elevated when you are in an actual fight or flight situation, like being chased by a tiger, not when you are stressed about whether your tax bill is high or not.

After about three minutes of my Sciencey Speech, my other friend / mentor / former client Nishant said, "Bro, why are you not recording this? This is really good content. And you just put it out there."

Seconds later, we took it LIVE, re-doing the whole speech.

And we got over 1,000 views on the first night.

I kept it up. It takes me 3-6 minutes to do a live video. I get about 1-3 client applications per LIVE video. It is so easy and takes little to no time. Why would I not do it?

As I progressed, I got better at my headline copy, and got more views. I got better at relating to my audience, and got even more views. I learned how to structure my pitch, set the scene, break complex subjects down, ask for shares, get likes, and even do a power call-out directly to my audience. More views, more applications, more conversions.

Today I do 5-7 LIVE videos per week. It's crazy simple, costs no money, and makes money.

Why would you not do it???

My entire business runs on me and my business partner going LIVE. It's our engine.

Sure, we have extra money now to boost our content and pay for ads, but the LIVE content is the engine. It creates the momentum. Our company (not including my own personal coaching) now earns over $10,000 a month.

So yeah. You can either fail a bunch, hate yourself, live like a starving dog searching for food.

-or-

You can do the intelligent, simple, zero cost option. And change your life now.

It is so simple to do and the only thing that could actually hold you back is that you're scared? Since there is literally no legitimate excuse, why are YOU not going LIVE every day?

SECTION 3:
MONETIZING YOUR LIVE VIDEOS

Jenny⊙Live.com

Chapter 10:

Ways to Make Money on Live Video

Since livestreaming is still in its pioneering phase, it has yet to reach critical mass, and many ways to make money from livestreaming are still being created, developed and tested. In other words, the sky is the limit and more ideas are popping up every day.

1. Fan Donations

Some livestreaming platforms allow the viewers to donate money directly to the broadcaster through their app during the live feed. For example, YouTube has Super Chat, which gives creators a virtual tip jar by allowing viewers to contribute to broadcasters via a paid instant message or comment. The viewers purchase and send donations to the broadcaster through Super Chat. Periscope has a similar monetization model known as Super Hearts. Viewers are able to purchase packages of hearts ranging from $0.99 up to $100, with which they are then able to donate to the broadcasters of their choosing during the live feed.

There are also third-party apps that allow you to process donations from viewers through PayPal, credit cards, Skrill, Unitpay, and other payment options. One such app is Streamlabs, which supports over 20 languages and does not take fees from the tips received.

2. Advertising

Advertising is arguably the most conventional way to monetize livestreams, as we've all seen ads across all media platforms for decades. It seems like a straightforward solution- but it depends on your platform. Some platforms allow it, while others facilitate it, and still, others forbid it. Additionally, advertising on social platforms is regulated based on the size of audience and viewership you have.

For example: Facebook Live and Periscope allow pre-roll and mid-roll ads on their livestreams if you have a relatively large audience. (A pre-roll ad is a promotional video message played before the content that the viewer opted in to see. A mid-roll ad is like a pre-roll ad except in the middle of the chosen content.)

On YouTube, a creator can make money on their channel by volunteering to be a part of Google's AdSense once they reach 10,000 lifetime views.

It's always best to check the Terms of Service on each platform before running ads on your videos, especially in view of how quickly things change in this space.

3. Subscriptions

There are other websites, like Patreon, that allow fans and viewers to pay content creators a subscription amount of their choice in exchange for exclusive behind-the-scenes content. This allows creatives, performers, and content creators to generate a consistent income for creating the content that people love. Patreon boasts $150 million sent to creators monthly.

4. Affiliate Products

An affiliate is someone who has an agreement with a brand or business to promote their products or services using an "affiliate link" on their website and marketing efforts. In exchange, the company will pay the affiliate a portion of the sales generated by that referral.

When selling affiliate products through livestreaming, it will be important to have a link that is easy for viewers to remember. For example, rather than sending a viewer to **http://www.domainname.com/thisismyaffiliatelinkfort hebestbookever** it would be much better to use a URL shortener. Some URL shortener services are:

- Bit.ly
- Goo.gl
- TinyURL.com
- Ow.ly
- Bit.do

This could take an affiliate link from this:
http://www.domainname.com/thisismyaffiliatelinkfort hebestbookever
To this:
TinyURL.com/BestOfBooks
As you can see, the latter is much easier to remember for both the broadcaster and the viewer!

Another benefit to using a URL shortener service is that depending on the site and package option, you can track how many people used that specific link to get to your affiliate product, so you can collect data to fine tune your marketing strategy.

5. Sponsorships

A sponsorship is like advertising in the sense that you are promoting another business or product. The difference is that the company or brand becomes an official sponsor of your broadcasts, and in exchange for you becoming their ambassador they compensate you according to your contract terms.

SUCCESS STORY: Leslie Nance Goes from Cooking in Her Kitchen to National Sponsorships

Early on in my livestreaming adventures, I came across a fascinating woman who was being interviewed by a doctor on Blab. She was showing viewers how to make sauerkraut, and extolling the health benefits of making your own. It was during this time that I also had my daily interview show on Blab. I quickly did some recon on her, loved what I saw, and sent her an invitation to be on my show.

My show at the time was called "The Daily Q Show," and I interviewed people who demonstrated excellence in their field. Leslie Nance definitely fit the criteria!

What I discovered during my recon was that she beat breast cancer completely with food and nutrition, and she was on a mission to teach others what she had done. The way she was teaching others was through her blog and livestreaming. She had a daily show on Periscope called, "Lunch with Leslie," where she passionately taught people how to fall in love with their kitchen while changing their lifestyle to eat food that cancer cannot survive with. Her popular hashtag is #cancerhatesit, and as a Certified Holistic Cancer Coach, Leslie is not only changing the lives of others, but her livestreaming efforts are being noticed!

In 2017, Leslie was a finalist for a Shorty Award in the category, "Periscoper of the Year." Additionally, she has started a radio show with her husband, Robin Nance, called "Fork It Over" in her hometown of Ft. Collins, Colorado.

I met Leslie in person in January 2016 at Summit Live in San Francisco. Again, because of the livestreaming bond, we immediately greeted each other with a hug and couldn't seem to get enough time to hang out because the other 1,000+ attendees were hanging around. We did, however, squeeze together in the back seat of an Uber to get to the airport at the end of the convention, and to be honest, that was one of the highlights of my trip!

Leslie is leading the way in getting sponsors for her livestreaming shows. I asked her to share with us how she has done this and any tips and tricks we can learn from what she's done!

Monetizing is not for wimps!

A cancer journey spurred my decision to start my business. I needed to teach others what I had learned about making the body inhospitable to cancer. So I started go2kitchens.com. At first I thought I was going to be a YouTube star with a GoPro strapped to my head. I called myself "the hands" because that was all you could see. I was on the right track but the wrong train. Now "hands and pans" videos are everywhere.

After about five months of struggling to get my videos and website seen, my BFF told me about this app where you do your shows live. I won't lie- it seemed a bit nerve wracking to tell my story live with no editing safety net. I felt very naked and vulnerable the first time I hit that "go live" button. That was two years ago, and I have never looked back! Now I get paid to do my show. I have sponsors! To be honest, sometimes I feel like Lucille Ball in her Vita-Vita-Vegeman commercials!

I have some wisdom to share about getting big brands to pay attention to your livestreams, plus how to get them to pay you to do the work you are already doing for free.

Opposites do not attract when it comes to attracting brands. As a livestreamer specializing in healthy food, I cannot expect that Hersey's will come knocking any day now. I do not have their audience, and they do not have mine. You must identify brands that will benefit your message, and in turn you will add value to theirs. A match made in heaven is when you are a super fan of the brands you are attracting. You know and trust their products, and it is easy to convince your audience how wonderful they are.

Free love attracts the big brands! To negotiate killer deals with them, you do not need 100,000 Instagram live followers or 10,000 people visiting your livestreams. I only have 20,000 Twitter/Periscope followers, yet I have six national brands and a handful of small local businesses that sponsor my show "Lunch with Leslie." The key is to share a little free love with them. Here's how...

It's called the hash and tag dance! Do it well and you will lure them into watching your show by tagging them and using their own hashtags. Livestreaming is still so new they are interested in seeing how you are talking about them. They will show up when you give them the free love and devotion of being a super fan. Then they are willing to pay you to give them more and more love.

Once a big brand has shown up in your show, or even dropped a comment, drop them a line. Send a thoughtful email telling them how fantastic it was for them to show up in your show. Tell them how much you love them and that your audience is hooked on their products. You will get a reply- and do you know why? It's fan mail! When they reply, ask how they normally work with influencers and who is the best person to talk to about your live show. It works like a charm.

Be patient! It took me a year to land my biggest national brand. I pitched and pitched ideas. I thought all was lost. But yet again, I sent a follow-up email, and Boom! The contract arrived in my email three days later. However, keep in mind that although big corporations are hard to deal with, the bigger they are, the bigger budget they have.

One thing I learned with the big brands is that you need someone within the company to be assigned to your project. Ask up front whom that person will be, and make your contact think seriously about that end of the deal. Lots of brands are still new at influencer marketing, and they don't always have a staff member assigned to the project. This is where you can be proactive and ask that question!

A reason I like the smaller brands is because they are much easier and faster to work with than the larger ones.

I worked for just under two years building a powerful community. This community is the backbone of everything I do. It was always my goal to have my content be free to my viewers, and to have sponsors pay me for my work. Let's face it- if you are crazy popular and also flat broke, you have a hobby and not a business!

The brands are attracted to my community and engagement. They don't care that I don't have a million followers. They only care that I care about my community and that my community cares about me.

Once I get my foot in the door, I am always shocked at how willing the brands are to spend large sums of money. In one sponsored month of my show, I can make double what any of my viewer-based membership programs have paid me.

I guess this would be my last tip: Don't undersell yourself. You and your community are worth every penny. Ask for the sky and only negotiate a little because there is someone else waiting for your genius who is willing to pay you what you are worth.

I have gone from no income to a blossoming income, and growing every day. I get to work with amazing brands I love. I get to share free goodies with my community. Best of all, I am getting paid to do the work I was already doing for free!

Livestreaming is the blogging of the future. A livestreaming program that shares content in an authentic way is not only a brand's dream, it is also a venue where they are looking for genuine connections to their consumers. Be the link that connects all the dots together.

6. Your Own Products or Services

This seems to be the most obvious way to make money with livestreaming, and also the most challenging for many people. In my experience, people don't want to appear like a used car salesman or an infomercial pitching their wares while on live video. This is a valid concern and one that is worthy of attention.

There are two truths that are undeniable:
1. People need to make money, *but*
2. Their customers don't want to be "Sold"

For many people, this is a challenging balance to achieve. We know that livestreaming is all about building relationships, being authentic, giving value, and building the know, like, and trust factor. But what is this all for if we never ask for the sale?

This is an art in and of itself: to be able to go on live video, add value, engage with the viewers, and ask for the sale. It's so much of an art, in fact, that the entire next chapter is dedicated to it.

7. How to Ask for the Sale on Live Video

As I mentioned at the end of the previous section, selling on livestream is its own skillset to master. While I coach specifically on the skills, nuances, techniques and technical aspects of livestreaming, selling products or services on live video requires an additional set of skills.

I invited sales coach, colleague and friend Aandra Bohlen to share with us what she teaches her students when it comes to selling on live video. We met in New York City in September 2015 at the Periscope Community Summit. She has been a regular on my shows, sharing her gifts and insights with my audience.

One of the reasons that I really appreciate her style of selling is because it is assertive and clear, it is anti-sleazy, and it emphasizes building relationships and offering value to the whole person as the end customer. It is never about just making money; it is about offering something of value (your product or service) in exchange for something else of value (money).

Sell It Live

By now you know that leveraging livestreaming for your business will help you increase visibility, build authority, and provide a platform for you to make a transformational impact on the customers your business serves.

What if I told you it could also, absolutely, without a doubt, INCREASE YOUR SALES?!

Yes, it can!

We can do this by using the super simple ASK LADDER.

But before we get into this, there are four basic concepts you should know:

1. *If you don't sell your product or services, no one else will.*
2. *Selling is not sleazy: Selling is Serving.*
3. *Always have a Call-to-Action. Always.*
4. *Understand your viewers' Level of Risk.*

Before we can do that, let's just acknowledge that there are some negative stigmas around selling that need to be busted in order for you to step into a soulfully aligned and authentic sales practice for your business. Let's take a look at the most common stigma around selling:

Stigma #1 – Selling is sleazy (and you would rather barf in a bag than be perceived as a pushy, desperate, icky sales person)

Let's face it: The only reason why this is coming up is because you've experienced firsthand what it feels like to be pitched to without being heard, being shamed if you didn't buy, and not being told clearly how that offer would truly help you based on what you need to move yourself forward.

But this doesn't have to be you. What's amazing is that because of this experience you are perfectly positioned to show up differently and step into soulfully aligned and authentic sales practices!

This can be done when you:
- *Realize the transformational power of your products*
- *Realize exactly who your product serves*
- *Realize that your product is the perfect prescription for what is ailing your prospects*
- *Realize that your product is designed and built to SERVE*
- *Realize that if you won't speak up and be the voice of your products NO ONE ELSE WILL*

Remember the last time you attended a live presentation, and happily purchased a service/product? Clearly, you purchased because you realized the points above. You didn't feel sold, you felt SOUL'D: you knew that what they offered was the very thing that could help you go from where you were to where you wanted to be.

So how can you adopt this type of soulfully aligned and authentic sales practice on your livestreams? It's simple:

Start allowing your viewers the opportunity to hear how they can solve their problem through your offerings!

In fact, when you don't share what's available to them you are actually:

- *Leaving them in the dark*
- *Leaving them hanging out to dry*
- *Leaving them without a way to rid themselves of their pain*
- *Leaving them to find their solution SOMEWHERE ELSE, from someone who might not be trustworthy*

Think of it this way: **Selling is serving!**

The next thing to understand is the Call-to-Action.

A Call-to-Action is simply asking your audience to do something. For example, it can be asking them to:

- *Like your page*
- *Join your group/subscribe to your blog*
- *Click on a link to a free resource*
- *Click on a link to purchase*

You want to do this because you want your audience to know up front that there is always an exchange of some sort for the valuable free content you are sharing via your livestream. This makes it clear to your audience that you're in business and they will respect and appreciate knowing how you operate and the way you work.

And guess what? People love this! They love to 'pay for what they receive.' This is called RECIPROCITY and we are wired to pay for what we value. Whether we pay in likes, clicks, or in cash, all of that is considered compensation!

Now about your viewers' Level of Risk. When a viewer hears a Call-to-Action, the internal question they are asking themselves is: 1) What does it 'cost' them to take your action, and 2) Is the reward higher than the risk? If the reward is clearly higher than the risk, then you are going to get more action, more conversion, and more sales! Cha-Ching!

There are three basic levels of risk.

__Low risk – high reward__: Doesn't expose them personally, and doesn't cost them a lot of time in exchange for the ask.

- *Like my page*
- *Subscribe to my bot to get notifications*
- *Join my group*
- *Check out this blog*
- *No opt-in-required resource*

- *No opt-in-required freebie*

Medium risk – high reward: *Exposes them slightly personally, and costs a minimal amount of time in exchange for the ask.*
- *Opt-in for free resource*
- *Opt-in for access to group*
- *Opt-in for mini training*
- *Pay under $10 for product/service/training*

Higher risk – high reward: *Exposes them more personally (financially), and costs more time in exchange for the ask.*
- *Anything that costs money and carries a longer time commitment from them*

NOW you have the tools to use the ASK LADDER.

You are now including a Call-to-Action in every livestream, right? Simply start with the Lower Risk-High Reward calls-to-action, and then every 2-3 livestreams, 'Ask' them up to the next step of the 'Ladder' of higher rewards.

For example:

1. *Select a specific product or service you would like to pitch on your livestream.*

2. *Create three Calls-to-Action:*
    a. *Low Risk – High Reward (such as following your page so they get updates)*
    b. *Medium Risk – High Reward (such as opting in for free information, or joining your group, or investing $2.99 in an informative e-book you've written)*
    c. *Higher Risk – High Reward (such as the three-day training you are offering, or a coaching contract)*

3. *For 2-3 livestreams, include your Low Risk offer in your Call-to-Action.*

4. *Then, for the next 2-3 livestreams, include your Medium Risk offer in your Call-to-Action.*

5. *Finally, for the next 2-3 livestreams, include your Higher Risk offer in your Call-to-Action.*

6. *Repeat this process for each specific product or service you would like to offer.*

Now that you know why selling is really how you can show up in true service to your business and those it serves, and you have a simple way to get your sales party started on livestreaming, conducting your sales conversations from an authentically aligned and soulful place, there's only one thing left to do: Go out and get your sell on!

SECTION 1:
WHAT, WHY, WHO, AND WHERE OF LIVESTREAMING

Jenny☑Live.com

What's Next?

All of the information I've shared with you has taken me over two years of intense immersion to learn. I imagine it is pretty overwhelming at this point. Does it feel like getting started in livestreaming is a daunting task?

I can assure you that taking it one step at a time is the way to go, and before you know it, you'll be livestreaming like a pro! (Yes, I know it's a cheesy rhyme, but I'm going with it.)

Everything we've ever learned seems overwhelming until we know it. Have you ever watched a baby learn to walk? The baby falls down countless times, but each time, gets back up to try again.

It's the same with a teenager learning to drive. It can be agonizing to observe, and often scary, as a new driver takes the wheel and accelerates the gas. But, with enough practice, driving becomes an automated task.

The same is true with livestreaming. When you take it step-by-step and implement the steps in order, practicing as often as you can, before you know it, you really will be livestreaming like a pro.

On your journey, I have a few resources for you, and a tip or two.

1. You can ALWAYS reach out to me with a question. You can find me on both Twitter and Facebook as "JennyQ"

2. Join my private livestreaming Facebook "Go Live! Insiders Community" where we share livestreaming news, tips, and tricks, simply go to: http://Facebook.JennyQ.Live

3. Tons of free info over at http://JennyQLive.com

4. Remember, your first 100 broadcasts are going to suck. (Probably not 100, and probably not totally suck.) That's OKAY! Get started. Don't quit.

5. As you're learning, be kind to yourself. You wouldn't berate a baby learning to walk or a teenager learning to drive, would you? (Okay, don't answer the latter). Remember to ask yourself after each broadcast, "What went well? What could have gone better?" Even if your answer for "What went well?" is "I hit the GO LIVE button," then celebrate that! You're way ahead of the game simply by taking that action!

I know you can do this, and I can't wait to see what you create! Please feel free to tag me in your live videos, or use the hashtag #JennyQLive so I can see it!

And, I end this book as I end every broadcast:

Live Well.
Have Fun.
Love Others.

xoxo JennyQ

Acknowledgments

As I sit to write acknowledgements, I am filled with gratitude. I feel so lucky to get to do what I do and with such incredible people.

I'd like to thank Terilee Harrison and the team at WIPublish for helping me get this book out of my head and onto paper. Additionally, I'd like to thank my amazing editors and proofreaders for their countless hours of editing, without which this book would not have gone to publication; no way, no how. Also, thanks to Tiffany for the incredible cover design and her patience, as I sent change after change after change. Each with an immediate deadline.

A journey of any success is never about one person. It's about a million exchanges, countless words of encouragement, and endless sharing of ideas.

This book is a result of learning a skill shoulder-to-shoulder with the incredible people in the livestreaming community. Along the way, many of them have taught me, helped me, and encouraged me. To be able to name them individually would be a nearly impossible task, and in trying to do so, I fear I would leave someone out who truly deserves to be thanked! Suffice it to say that *without my livestreaming friends, colleagues, and cohorts, this journey would not have been nearly as rewarding, fun, or exciting!*

And the viewers - THE VIEWERS!! You may have thought that I was giving you something by creating content, but to be clear, it was my life that has been enriched. Not one like, comment, share, tweet, private message, email, or virtual heart on my livestream broadcasts has gone unnoticed. There were days that I questioned if I should keep going, then magically someone would send me an email with a "Great job!" or a text "Thank you for sharing your journey!" or a private message "Thank you for that show, it helped me with something I'm struggling with!"

I would also like to thank *each guest* who came on my show and shared their time, wisdom, and insight with my audience. Personally, after each interview I was left feeling more inspired and motivated to be more, do more, and give more.

A HUGE thank you to my friends who contributed their stories, successes, and experiences to this book! There is nothing quite like real-life examples and I thank you for yours! Namely: Leslie Nance, Ross Brand, Hilary Silver, Mitch Jackson, Aandra Bohlen, John Kapos, and Glenn Dawson.

MY TRIBES! I feel beyond fortunate to have found not one, but two groups of "my people" who truly keep me focused, grounded, and inspired!

Women Ignite International – To all the women on the core leadership team and the Igniters – I've never known a group of women who can truly support, encourage, and inspire each other with so much love and light.

H2HClub and H2H Marketing Hub — This human to human movement attracts the best of the best. Consistently learning together, pushing each other, and sharing knowledge — my heart is full of gratitude. Thank you to Bryan & Courtney for the vision and leading the way!

Julie Babcock-Hyde — Long-time friend, colleague, darn good CPA, and the ever-present voice of reason who always finds a way to diplomatically tell me what I need to hear and not necessarily what I want to hear. Your support through the years has meant more than you probably realize. Until now, maybe. Maybe now you do.

Sheli Gartman — It's not every day I find someone who can give me a run for my money in the areas of energy, fun, ideas, and ambition. But then you came along! You have a way of making me see how even though it's not a perfect world, it's pretty amazing to be here! Thank you for believing in me and showing it in word and action. I'm keeping you.

Tobe Brockner – Even though you thought there was a chance I was crazy for investing so much time in livestreaming (see Introduction), you encouraged my vision in those early days when no logic backed it up. It's possible (probable) that without your support of "The Daily Q Show" this book wouldn't exist.

Glenn Dawson – Thanks for coaching me and pushing me beyond anything I knew was possible. Not just as a personal trainer, but in life and business. How'd such a young punk get so smart, anyway?

#Top5MostInfluentialPeopleInMyLife

Dave Lakhani – Thank you for asking the hard and thought-provoking questions, having no judgement on the answers, and offering invaluable feedback and direction. Your direct approach is, well, bold. And it is so effective in helping me more clearly define my goals, values, and self.

My lifelong besties - Shelly, Michele, Angela - The ones who consistently remind me where I came from, who I am, and how far I can go - I CHERISH YOU!!

Saving the best for last...

My family – being the youngest of six, we have a big one! My sisters and brothers have always encouraged me to be the best I can! A slew of nephews and nieces that I consider to be friends! Thank you for not only always being there for me, but also for standing by me for those first seven months of livestreaming when I became so completely immersed that I might have missed a few seasonal weather changes. Thank you for always being my biggest and loudest cheerleaders!

My greatest inspirations are also my favorite people ever. Rachel, Nicole, Vit, Brian, and Gabrielle – you are, and will always be, my greatest accomplishment! Thank you for your endless encouragement, support, and love. Everything I do is in hopes of having you proud to say, "That's my Mom!"

And last, but certainly not least, Jon -- from the first time I hit "Start Broadcast" to the moment the final draft was sent to the publisher, none of this would have been possible without your support. From the deepest part of my heart, *Thank You*.

Resources

In this section I've listed helpful resources along with contact info for all my friends who shared their stories, knowledge, and experiences in this book. I'm pretty sure after hearing about them, you are going to want to start watching their broadcasts!

Aandra Bohlen – Sales Coach – Creator of Sell it LIVE
https://aandrabohlen.com/

Glenn Dawson – Online Personal Trainer
https://www.facebook.com/resetufitness/

H2HClub – Marketing Club to Master All Areas of Marketing
http://www.h2hclub.com/

Jennifer Quinn

Hilary Silver – Relationship Expert / Coach / Consultant
http://www.hilarysilver.com/

John Kapos – 3rd Generation Chocolatier
http://perfectionchocolates.com.au/

Leslie Nance – Certified Holistic Cancer Coach
http://www.go2kitchens.com/

Mitch Jackson – California lawyer, Tech Entrepreneur
https://streaming.lawyer/

Ross Brand – Founder, LivestreamUniverse
http://livestreamuniverse.com/

ABOUT THE AUTHOR

Jennifer Quinn is a livestreaming expert, coach, speaker, and trainer. She has owned and operated a digital marketing company since 2007. Along with her team, Jennifer has helped hundreds of small businesses owners claim their presence online. In 2008, she fell in love with Twitter. JennyQ marveled at how genuine connections were made through 140-character tweets.

Once Jennifer discovered livestreaming, she decided to dive full-force into this emerging technology. She quickly built up a following and was recently ranked by Klout as the #2 livestreaming expert worldwide. JennyQ loves to "geek out" about technology; especially livestreaming, augmented reality and virtual reality.

Always inquisitive and rarely satisfied – JennyQ loves to discover why people do what they do. Social media and livestreaming have helped her find out what makes people tick. *The JennyQ Show*, which started out with interviewing people who have demonstrated excellence in their fields, evolved into a full-blown variety show.

During her live show, she's not afraid to ask people the hard questions. She wants to know what truly drives people, not just the surface level answers.

The JennyQ Show has covered topics geared towards small businesses, entrepreneurs and solopreneurs. She's interviewed:

➢ **don Miguel Ruiz, Jr.**, Best-selling author of "The Five Levels of Attachment."
➢ **Kim Coles**, actress & comedienne of In Living Color & Living Single
➢ **Bob Burg**, co-author of "The Go-Giver" books
➢ **Judge Alex**, from the Judge Alex TV Show
➢ **Robert Scoble**, author, tech influencer, blog "Scobleizer"

Jennifer chose Boise, Idaho as her home after traveling the world as a military spouse. She is a transformation enthusiast, self-proclaimed music addict, and coffee lover.

What you'll find at: http://JennyQLive.com

- Keynote speaker topics / contact info
- One-on-one livestream coaching
- Video digital courses – learn at your own pace
- Group livestream coaching
- Equipment & gear
- Free tips & tricks for livestreaming
- And more!!

How to contact Jennifer directly:
Facebook:
http://facebook.com/TheJennyQShow
Twitter:
http://twitter.com/JennyQ
Join her livestreaming Facebook Community:
https://www.facebook.com/groups/GoLiveCommunity/

THIS BOOK IS PROUDLY PUBLISHED BY WIPUBLISH,
A DIVISION OF WOMEN IGNITE INTERNATIONAL.

Contact: Terilee Harrison, Director
terilee@womenigniteinternational.com

www.womenigniteinternational.com
LIKE us on Facebook: www.facebook.com/wipublish

✓ **Live Well.**
☺ **Have Fun.**
♥ **Love Others.**

$19.95

ISBN 978-0-9852699-1-3

51995>

9 780985 269913

Made in the USA
Lexington, KY
08 October 2018